GUILTY PLEASURES

by Alan Britt

Access Road Studios
Wilbraham, Massachusetts 01095
USA

Copyright © 2022 by Alan Britt

First Edition

All rights reserved.

No part of this book may be used or reproduced in any manner whatsoever without written permission except in the case of brief quotations embodied in critical articles or reviews.

Front cover art: "Catwoman" by Mel Ramos: Lithograph 32"x 29" (collection of the artist)

Back cover art: "Mel Ramos Swimming" by Gabriel Navar

Cover design and book design by:

Ricardo Fonseca
American B Graphics, LLC
American-B-Graphics.com

Kevin Bartolotti
Blue Glory Graphics, LLC
BlueGloryGraphics.com

ISBN-13: 978-1-7370339-0-5

Available at independent bookstores and from Magical Jeep Distributing: www.magicaljeep.com/shop/britt/10

Manufactured in the United States of America.

10 9 8 7 6 5 4 3 2 1

GUILTY PLEASURES

ACKNOWLEDGEMENTS

The poems (sometimes in earlier versions) in this book appeared in the following publications. Grateful acknowledgement is made to the editors of those publications:

Alternative Reel (Poet's Corner): "After a Rainstorm," "Scarlet Spider," "Tiny Magenta Spiders," "White Butterflies," and "July, 2002: Teeth of Nomenclature"

Ann Arbor Review: "Ode to a West Nile Mosquito," "Ode to a Female Cardinal and a Harley," "Age Three," and "Ode to an Incense Tile"

Ashvamegh…The Literary Flight (India): "Ode to Paradox"

The Bitter Oleander: "September Is a Good Month for Shiraz"

Blue & Yellow Dog: "Ode to Amnesia," "Ode to the Echo of Shelley," "Ode to a Dream," and "Ode to a Brown Widow"

The Cultural Journal: "Ode to a Car Alarm" and "Circular Ode"

Darkling: "Ode to Shasta," "September Is a Good Month for Shiraz," "Nonsense Ode," and "Confronted by a Question with Ebony Eyes"

Deep Tissue Magazine: "Manna," "Geronimo's Cadillac," "Ode to Guilty Pleasures," "Ode to Cracker," and "Ode to Silliness"

English Journal: "Ode to Langston Hughes" and "Ode to Gnats"

Exercise Bowler: "For Eddie" and "A Hummingbird"

Illya's Honey: "Habana, Cuba"

Jelleyfish Whispers: "Ode to a Common Spider, Greyish-Brown with Zebra Suspenders" and "The Bee"

New Gravity: "Ode to Misery," "Ode to an Incense Tile," and "Ode to a Flamenco Dancer"

Prick of the Spindle: "Ode to Freedom"

Pyrokinection: "Poet Talking to the Wind" and "October Evening"

Red Fez: "Ode to Truth"

Refined Savage Poetry Review: "Ode to Nothing"

Sprindrift: "Ode to September," "Ode to a Sable Cricket," and "Ode to a Fragment"

Straitjackets: "Ode to Paradox," "Ode to Love," "Varietal Ode," and "Ode to Thoughts"

13th Warrior Review: "Ode to 1958"

* * * * * * * *

"The Intuitive Soul," interview/essay (translated into Romanian by Ruxandra Cesereanu) in *Steaua*, Cluj, Transylvania, Romania: 2002

"The Intuitive Soul," (interview/essay) in *Pijin: Online Magazine of Poetry & Fiction*: 2003

"Ode to Velázquez" in *The Gothic: New Jersey City University's Alumni Magazine*, New Jersey City University, Spring: 2003

"Nonsense Ode" in *International Gallerie's* issue "Migration: When the Boats Go To and Fro," Vol 19. No 1, Bina Sarkar Ellias, Editor, Mumbai, India, September 2016

"Ode to Langston Hughes" in *Time of the Poet Republic*, Mbizo Chirasha, Editor/Publisher, Miombopublishing, Zimbabwe: June, 2020

* * * * * * * *

"Ode to Velázquez" in *Ekphrastia Gone Wild Anthology* edited by Rick Lupert, Ain't Got No Press, Los Angeles: 2013

* * * * * * * *

"Ode to September," "Ode to Velázquez," "Ode to Guilty Pleasures," "Ode to Maple Seeds," "Ode to 1958," "Ode to Paradox," and "Ode to Langston Hughes" in *Parabola Dreams: Poems by Silvia Scheibli and Alan Britt*, The Bitter Oleander Press, Fayetteville, NY: 2013

* * * * * * * *

"Ode to Nothing" in *Ode to Nothing/Óda a semmihez* by Alan Britt, English/Hungarian, (translated into Hungarian by Paul Sohar), published by Iniquity Press/Vendetta Books in Cooperation with Concord Media Jelen (Irodalmi Jelen), Arad, Romania [Irodalmi Jelen könyvek, Zoltán Böszörményi, Publisher]: 2018

DEDICATION

Appreciation to those who offered encouragement and support throughout the writing of this book: Steve Barfield, Zoltán Böszörményi, Mary Beth Britt, Heath Brougher, Paula Gottschalk, Charles P. Hayes, Dzvinia Orlowsky, José Rodeiro, Paul B. Roth, Silvia Scheibli, and Paul Sohar

Also, to Stephen Sleboda for his patience and unerring support for this project

Particular appreciation to Rochelle Ramos Leininger for generous assistance with her father's front cover artwork for this book and to Gabriel Navar for providing the back cover artwork

Finally, to the late great California Pop Art pioneer Mel Ramos whose courageous and vivid art from the 1960s onward continues to grace the walls of major museums throughout the world

"Air Mail" by Mel Ramos

Contents

- 1 -

Foreward by José Rodeiro..x
After a Rainstorm..13
Scarlet Spider..14
Tiny Magenta Spiders..15
White Butterflies...16
July, 2002: Teeth of Nomenclature.......................................17
Habanna, Cuba...18
Manna...19
Geronimo's Cadillac...20
For Eddie...22
Ode to Shasta...23
September Is a Good Month for Shiraz....................................24
Ode to September..25
Nonsense Ode..26
Confronted by a Question with Ebony Eyes................................28

- 2 -

Hummingbird...31
Ode to Velázquez..32
Ode to Guilty Pleasures...33
Ode to Cracker..34
Ode to a West Nile Mosquito...35
Ode to a Female Cardinal and a Harley...................................36
Ode to Silliness..37
Ode to a Sable Cricket..38
Ode to Maple Seeds..39
Ode to a Car Alarm..40
Circular Ode..41

- 3 -

Ode to a Fragment...45

Ode to Misery 46
Ode to a Common Spider, Charcoal-Brown with Zebra
　　Suspenders. 47
Ode to an Incense Tile. 48
Ode to a Flamenco Dancer 49
The Bee 50
Age Three 51
Poet Talking to the Wind 52
October Evening. 53
Ode to Freedom 54
Ode to 1958 55

– 4 –

Ode to Paradox. 59
Ode to Truth 60
Ode to Love 61
Varietal Ode 62
Ode to Thoughts 63
Ode to Langston Hughes 64
Ode to Amnesia. 65
Ode to the Echo of Shelley. 66
Ode to a Dream. 67
Ode to a Brown Widow. 68
Ode to Gnats 69

– 5 –

Ode to Nothing. 73

– 6 –

The Intuitive Soul (Interview/Essay). 95

Notes. 98
Bios 100
Publications 104

Foreword
by José Rodeiro

Alan Britt's *Guilty Pleasures* gallantly stands as an intrinsic and immanent coast-to-coast visual artistic and poetic collaboration between two strong image-based American Bay-oriented art scenes: Mel Ramos & Gabriel Navar's celebrated San Francisco Bay Oakland-*demimonde* and Alan Britt's ethereal Baltimore on the Chesapeake Bay. In fact, each poem's timely subject matter along with Ramos' "Catwoman" cover painting and Navar's "Mel Ramos Swimming" back cover painting evoke all the dynamic whirlwind of contemporary America, seductively arousing a deep apprehension of the human condition where, e.g., in Britt's breezy poem dedicated to Ramos, "Poet Talking to the Wind," a mere gust can disarray and disrobe each being's lonely Heideggerian apprehension of the viewer's *Dasein* paradox.

The wind flips her walnut curls—she's aware
that coffins of avocados taste like a delicious
chimera of impossibilities. So, upon departing,

she feigns that she's forgotten something
of value, something primordial, something
religious, perhaps, while rummaging her

lilac shoulder bag just in time to witness
Eve ascending nude from a Reese's peanut
butter bar like a Cnidian Venus rising.

Britt's literary feats of sheer primordial poesy furnish briming symbolic Blakean metaphoric word feasts infused with both expansive imagery as well as an array of subtle embedded images that forge complex imagery from imaginative visual perceptions enthused to overpower and question mere cerebral comprehension.

Like all guilty pleasures, Britt's *Guilty Pleasures* begins resplendently with the poem "After a Rainstorm" wherein assorted birds (a sparrow, finches, ravens, cardinals, robins, and warblers) frantically converse after an evening rainstorm. From that point on, you cannot stop reading until you arrive at the crescendo (orgasm) of Britt's anti-epic "Ode to Nothing."

~José Rodeiro, Visual Artist's Fellow in Painting,
National Endowment for the Arts, Washington, DC.
Art Editor, *RAGAZINE.CC.* 2011-2017

1

*I no longer love her, that's certain, but maybe I love her.
Love is so short, forgetting is so long.*

~Pablo Neruda
(trans. by W.S. Merwin)

AFTER A RAINSTORM

After a rainstorm,
a white-throated sparrow,
cucumber flower tucked
behind her left ear,
addresses the neighborhood.

Cool July breeze.

Finches chatter.

Ruby spider, smaller than
a pinhead, wobbles my eyelash.

Twenty feet away two ravens
take turns
sawing the dusk
into onion skin slices.

Blazing cardinal and saffron
robin intervene with twisted
whistles and bruised warbles,
while two erudite ravens, unabashed,
whittle away at leftover sunlight.

SCARLET SPIDER

Cicada rattles
right before
crickets explode
from damp July weeds.

Hound dog barks
resemble a hammer
on plywood
inside
a hollow shed.

Scarlet spider,
smaller than
a flea,
scurries
the Kuiper Belt
of this poem.

TINY MAGENTA SPIDERS

Relaxing beneath my umbrella maple
for six minutes and already
one hundred tiny magenta spiders
come crawling through my hair!

Tiniest magenta spiders
parachute by the dozens
onto my blueblack checkered drawstrings,
onto my poem,
and into my Australian chardonnay
with beads of sweat
trickling its guava waist.

These spiders resemble pinpoints of ruby
fur scurrying on eight invisible legs.

They're beautiful
and totally oblivious
to my infatuation
for them.

In bed at night I think of them while itching
places I normally wouldn't contemplate
before falling asleep.

WHITE BUTTERFLIES

Two cabbage butterflies, furious about something,
weave a white tornado above the taffeta tendrils

of summer forsythia while tangoing past basil
and mint plus cucumber vines grieving their

galvanized cages before swirling an eggplant's
lavender tongue of sexual desire. Alas, it never

dawns upon them they could be lovers.

JULY, 2002: TEETH OF NOMENCLATURE

(For Duane Locke)

He wears a harness of green bells,
this poet I admire immensely.

Each bell
curls
and uncurls
like seahorses
led by White Mountain Apache scouts
through the dreadful years
of European occupation.

Each day this poet discovers new bells,
lost bells, rusted and dented bells
disguised as alleyway trash
abandoned exquisitely,
ironically,
beneath the orthodontic teeth
of nomenclature.

HABANA, CUBA

Wind's Jezebel fingernails waltz
around the moonlit wrought iron
rails of Habana's gilded balconies—
balconies built by an ivory ball
tripping the red and the black while
stumbling past, as it were, the
cancerous lump in Batista's throat.

MANNA

Pulverize the carrots, add beets, banana,
celery, kale, one organic apple, plus a knuckle
of ginger into a slurry of oat milk.

Guzzle the entire mix.

This juice will revive you from the dead,
will merge you with the One so that you
too may become a banana frond's bruised
shoulder blade sheltering a giant vermilion
and tobacco grasshopper with diminutive
drops of rust for eyes.

This juice will alert you to tamarind
seeds shaken inside plastic crucifixes
by infants rocking in their cradles.

Indeed, this juice will sustain you
through agony and doubt.

Oh, yes, almost forgot, make sure to
include a wild poem as your holy biscuit
with every cup of this marvelous juice.

GERONIMO'S CADILLAC

(They took Old Geronimo by storm,
and ripped off the feathers from his uniform.
They stole his land, now they won't give it back,
and gave Geronimo a Cadillac.)
         (~sung by Johnny Rivers)

Geronimo squats on a rock
overhanging a cliff
in mythical darkness

to contemplate stars'
dandelion trails
crisscrossing the universe.

Oh, now, take me back,
I wanna ride in Geronimo's Cadillac.

Later, Geronimo sells his autograph
at St. Louis World's Fair, 1904,
for 25¢ a pop, plus cabinet card

photographs of himself, along
with autographed blankets, ponchos
and quivers for non-Apaches.

But, tonight, a southwest wind nips
the Appaloosa flanks
of an October moon

in Juarez, Mexico,
as it always has
and always will.

*Oh, now, take me back,
I wanna ride in Geronimo's Cadillac.*

*Oh, now, take me back,
I wanna ride in Geronimo's Cadillac.*

[Italicized lyrics by Michael Murphey and Charles Quarto]

FOR EDDIE

As the *Raven* said, poems make sad companions.

Sometimes true, Eddie, as your auntie called you.

In fact, just yesterday, cellphones, school busses and
fire alarms haunted my fifty-two-year-old brain juggling
an obsidian and cobalt blue swallowtail, plus hollow
cicada husks resembling empty walnut shells anchored
to the exhausted roots of an Eastern Shore Wye Oak.

But at this very moment, back in Reisterstown, Maryland,
a poem rises from her ivory chaise lounge, faces me,
then trails the backs of her long jade fingernails through the
smoky locks lining both sides of my temples before diving
deep below the empty wells of my eyes.

ODE TO SHASTA

(For Shasta Vida Britt: 1987-2002)

I cover the wind's bony shoulders
with a coral-colored bath towel,

and together we enjoy a glass or two
of Southeastern Australian shiraz.

But the shoulders of this young wine
are more muscular than the shoulders

of the dying wind and so, eventually,
these shiraz shoulders swirl me

into each of Johann Strauss's 473
waltzes where large black crickets,

engorged on humidity, become ninjas
this first day of September until, later,

the wind, reduced now to the hollow
bones of catbirds and mockingbirds

that adore her, drags one paw across
the late season clover and, finally,

totters the back porch steps already
collapsing beneath the ashes of her soul.

SEPTEMBER IS A GOOD MONTH FOR SHIRAZ

Crows on this chilly overcast September afternoon
are large chunks of hail rattling the nearby maples.

Some crickets, fat and glistening black Baroque violins,
chirp so loud they erect a magnetic force around the
northern perimeter of imagination.

Green maples hiss, knowing what's ahead.

A motor scooter, like a water skier over cubes of ice,
wobbles our neighborhood side street.

A downy woodpecker threads her needle of consciousness
through the collapsed vein of this chilly afternoon.

An olive wind from the south, wearing turquoise anklets,
sterling bracelets, and a necklace made of sin, drags her
empty suitcase across September's yellow waist.

ODE TO SEPTEMBER

Chilly cloud's white manta belly
undulates the gunmetal sky,
if you're down
looking up.

Nearby ambulance displays ivory teeth
and bad disposition.

Volunteer fire alarm ignites
sleepy neighborhood's match head
before gradually burning down.

Crows leave hairline cracks
in the overcast afternoon.

Their atonal squawks
sprinkle ashes
over the porcelain shoulder blades
of my dreaming patio chair.

NONSENSE ODE

Our yard gets ragged around the edges
as it must in order to sustain
three families of squirrels, the annual
migration of straw-colored grasshoppers,
leopard slugs, and swallowtail ashes
of burnt amber.

There's a botanist's dream
happening above and between
the thick ribs of a split-rail fence
whose rose-of-Sharon
sweeps her lavender eyelashes
across tall wet weeds.

A woman dressed in shiraz taffeta
slinky gown
orders mezcal.

Maple leaves are dying to be limes
in this ode,
but their fate is sealed.

Blue jays burglarize hand tools
from a nearby shed.

The wind is Uma Thurman, tonight;
her glistening eyes recall Marlena Dietrich
slinking a white mink down the ebony
banister of an anaconda staircase.

The wind invades fluorescent patios
along the dappled kapok banks
of the Amazon.

The wind opens her hand
to reveal a compressed ruby
of Italian philosophy.

Apple trees in Copenhagen
produce apples pure white as the skins
of Spanish saints stretched across golden
crosses in Rococo cathedrals.

In Barcelona the crosses are frozen;
a film of ice surrounds their golden eternity
where an old woman, eyes waltzing
with distant planets, chips away
at the thick ice.

CONFRONTED BY A QUESTION WITH EBONY EYES

(For Paula Gottschalk)

With eyes like baseballs this question approaches me
down the creaky narrow wooden staircase
of an asparagus clapboard house
off snowy Williamsburg Pike
near Richmond, Indiana.

This question lifts the black iron door to the coal cellar
and funnels down a large pile of briquettes hauled
from a mine in Bluefield, West Virginia, a mine
that suffered its worst cave-in twelve years earlier.

It's September, 1954.

Coal falls with a soft intelligence,
in a lexicon I cannot decipher.

But, today, the arms of this question become zebra
butterflies flickering like ashes through sunlit shadows
before vaporizing behind the smoky branches
of death's favorite ornamental cherry tree.

2

I love
all
things,
not because they are
passionate
or sweet-smelling
but because,
I don't know,
because
this ocean is yours,
and mine.

~Pablo Neruda
(trans. by Ken Krabbenhoft)

HUMMINGBIRD

Hummingbird's emerald flame
flashes golden bell to golden bell
above sapphire vines constricting
the waist of a split-rail fence.

She traverses a switchblade
of sunlight that ignites forsythia
above the quicksilver fence.

Her feathers quiver jade photons
as she crosses this valley of sunlight
before vanishing behind a golden bell
for another sixteen hundred years.

ODE TO VELÁZQUEZ

(For José Rodeiro)

A painter posing before the beveled mirror
of a bustling palace
has the dark look of curious confidence.

Nearby
women flow
across the parquet palace floor.

All the satin worn that day
must've been worth thousands,
perhaps millions by today's standard.

Velázquez brushes plum blossoms
from the sultry lap
of daily royal existence.

He faces the mirror,
then steps through 500 years to smell
Cuban coffee brewing in José's kitchen.

ODE TO GUILTY PLEASURES

Guilty pleasures row gondolas
through moonlight's nightgown
rippling a canal's bare shoulders.

Cicadas and nightjars chatter.

Stars etch jellyfish light
across the sultry August sky.

Golden tomatoes moan.

Crickets, resembling large drops
of crude, extract magnesium kisses
from night's humid torso.

ODE TO CRACKER

My mother says he was a cocker spaniel,
my brother says a beagle,
but I'm telling you,
Cracker was a full-blooded Irish setter!

We bombed the place, had him flea dipped,
and still he transgressed Tuscaloosa Avenue,
ending up at a neighbor's house or the pound.

Each time Cracker was retrieved with promise
of collar and a tag.

But this dog had a legitimate sense that he
deserved better, starting with long intimate
walks, regular hours, and, for god's sake,
proper breed identification.

Regarding this last detail and not one
to give up easily, my older brother offers:
*Well, if this is the worst catastrophe
our family ever has to suffer!*

ODE TO A WEST NILE MOSQUITO

This ankle is not for sale,
my friend,
even as you crinkle
your pubic hair legs
against my white cotton sock,
incognito.

You see, Nilly, I'm wise
to your shenanigans
of pulling blood through a tube.

Still, this is not how I quench
my imagination,
or my iguana soul,
for that matter,
clinging to its barnacled rock
of lost faith.

ODE TO A FEMALE CARDINAL AND A HARLEY

Female cardinal, tawny,
scarlet eyeliner, scarlet tiara,
onyx eyeshadow,
cracked leather jacket,
eyes me intently
each time she pulls
ruby berries
from a wild vine crumbling
over a split-rail fence.

She monitors my every movement,
then hops across wet vines
and berries, shades of wintergreen
and burnt cherry, before vanishing
like a magician's silk handkerchief.

John Keats sits beside me,
writing a letter to someone.

I want to ask young John
about his nightingale, his Greek lovers,
plus, melancholy Autumn sprawled
across a granary floor.

But he owes letters, it seems,
to everyone in London.

Then the female cardinal returns
with flaming beak,
cinnamon-dusted shoulder blades,
and two long narrow tail feathers
like scarlet exhaust pipes hugging
the muscular thighs of a Harley.

ODE TO SILLINESS

All the birds of our neighborhood
commune in my backyard today.

They've commenced a meeting of some kind
and seem to be directing their irritation at me,
estranged as I am to their demands.

If only I could discern their agenda,
I might at least alleviate a modicum
of their distress.

But, alas, they bicker and babble, quibble
and quarrel, and all at the same time.

It's like being married, for god's sake.

No wonder I don't understand
one damn thing they're saying!

ODE TO A SABLE CRICKET

A large sable cricket
sings his ode.

He hammers and chisels,
half-hour or more,
creating
a cricket commentary
on daily existence,
including poignant remarks
about religion.

But this gorgeous cricket,
in his single-minded quest
for existential lucidity,
has around 4,000 religions
to choose from
but only a month or so
to make up his mind.

ODE TO MAPLE SEEDS

(For Michelangelo Buonarroti)

Maple seeds fall to the ground,
spiraling toward their heaven
that determines whether
they flourish
into full-grown maple trees
or disperse their atoms
for alternate purposes.

Same thing for humans,
only we float skyward
to our heaven,
which we'll never see
and never apprehend.

ODE TO A CAR ALARM

Scallop shell
sprung open—
death hinged at the back
of its throat.

CIRCULAR ODE

Maple leaves hiss
like the ocean
where I grew up
along the Atlantic—
muscular turquoise waves
assaulting
my ankles
and waist.

And, today, in my suburban
Maryland backyard,
the hiss of those distant
waves shivers maple leaves
braiding their banana-bitten
green ink-stained hair
above a galvanized
rain barrel.

3

In fact, the exterior landscape, becoming a mobile location, mobile in time and space, developed "multiple perspectives" and so became capable of serving as an interior landscape.

~E.S. Shaffer on Coleridge

ODE TO A FRAGMENT

Above giant oaks and poplars
fireworks splatter magenta
and green jellyfish tentacles
across a charcoal sky.

Crickets pound
humidity
below her chest.

One lone cicada shreds
bluewhite lamplight
into confetti.

While other cicadas echo
the receding hairline
of dusk.

ODE TO MISERY

It knocked scales off me,
living through all that.

So, these days I relax
and measure my pulse
against the throat of misery
while sipping cabernet
and watching a ceiling fan's
five beaver tails scatter
light through the
upside down crystal
tulips sagging
from the brass stems
of my kitchen chandelier.

ODE TO A COMMON SPIDER, CHARCOAL-BROWN WITH ZEBRA SUSPENDERS

There's this spider webbed
to our patio door.

Disappears, sleight-of-hand,
during routine human traffic.

Vanishes like the pea
in a NYC shell game!

Sure, I love his lust for freedom,
and emulate his fluid arachnid guile,
but, mostly, I'm jealous
of his endearing patience
for every fingernail moth of fate.

ODE TO AN INCENSE TILE

The incense tile is blind
as she scooches beside me
during my dream.

I don't know whether to fall
in love or to grow scales,
seeing as how it's all
a fairytale, anyway.

It's 2002, the season
for religious abuse,
so, I check my illusions at the altar
and stroll
the hollowed-out paradigms
of one thousand generations,
past lichen-covered philosophies
in search of a sober existence.

And just about then a wooden match
flickering its ladybug wings
sizzles the tip of one patchouli stick
that flashes like a lighthouse
before coughing up a lazy lotus
of blue smoke.

ODE TO A FLAMENCO DANCER

(For Anna Menendez)

This dancer—capricious—
shoulders covered with the crushed cloves
of tragic love affairs.

Eyelashes flutter their tamarind curtains
as violent heels rattle the wooden ceiling
of my feral imagination.

This dancer—audacious—
shoulders covered with the crushed cloves
of tragic love affairs.

THE BEE

So, this portly black bee
with dandelion suspenders
hoisting his hippopotamus rear
dances our encounter.

He conveys to other bees halfway across the yard:
Avoid this patio—the man sitting here is not a flower!

I wonder . . . my genteel Italian cologne,
or perhaps this faded sweatshirt recalling
wrinkled geranium petals fallen from grace?

Then, suddenly, like a drunken bullet,
this bee grazes my chin and vaporizes
inside a tropical disturbance
loitering the edge of our patio.

AGE THREE

The ancient philosopher tumbles
from his giant wooden rocking
horse into a vat of quicksilver.

Suddenly, it's the Tang Dynasty,
and he has about 64 years or so,
if he's lucky, to invent the water
clock and learn how to swim.

POET TALKING TO THE WIND

(For Mel Ramos)

The poet says to the wind, *Look inside that
black rose, inside atoms buzzing neon corollas,
inside that fist of roses shivering your breeze!*

Circling crows squeal like brakes
on a UPS truck hauling boxes addressed
in melancholy handwriting to no one

in particular. The wind invites the poet
to shift his waist against the chilly vinyl
straps of a Persian blue zero gravity chair.

I know, says the poet. *Whenever I recline, I dream
of impossibilities far outnumbering avocados
wrinkling wooden bins at the local farmer's market!*

The wind flips her walnut curls—she's aware
that coffins of avocados taste like a delicious
chimera of impossibilities. So, upon departing,

she feigns that she's forgotten something
of value, something primordial, something
religious, perhaps, while rummaging her

lilac shoulder bag just in time to witness
Eve ascending nude from a Reese's peanut
butter bar like a Cnidian Venus rising.

OCTOBER EVENING

With the clock ticking, the poet
begins losing his hearing
and his memory.

That's not fair!
Even Beethoven had memory!

So, one night the poet enters
a tavern and taps a saffron beer
bottle against the sentimental beat
of Country Western music
while recording every detail
of every pea soup tattoo sprawled
across every crinkled cleavage
slouching that dimly-lit bar.

And upon inhaling the smoky gazes
from each patron's eyes glistening
like thorny chameleons,
he feels like a fist!

ODE TO FREEDOM

> *So, that makes*
> *this chameleon a charlatan . . .*
> says the poet to a group of eager 3rd graders,
> *. . . he changes his skin*
> *whenever he's frightened!*

Children slowly raise their hands
and open their avocado eyes,
      while a moth,
    (sharing the poet's countenance),
        nibbles
   crude oil darkness
from a 16th century Rembrandt canvas
      before fluttering
           the icy glint
      of a tin ladle
        hanging
            in a cold
     late afternoon
         Dutch pantry.

ODE TO 1958

A disillusioned math teacher juggles egos
at the Palm Beach County Fair, 1958.

He flips torches,
eats fire,
then burns all the important papers
at the county courthouse.

The Lobster Man
and the Lobster Man's daughter
dine at a seafood restaurant
somewhere off Military Trail.

While my brother,
youngest polo player in the history
of Palm Beach County,
scores the winning goal
and achieves stardom
at the impressionable age of 16.

Then, poetry, ah, toughest teacher of them all,
stops by to share a cigarette, loosens silk buttons
lining her bloodstained blouse,
and breathes a wasp into Steve's left ear.

So, my brother discards his saddle,
lays down his bridle one last time,
and welcomes the eight arms of poetry's mystical
goddess to embrace just how elusive wisdom
can be without a web of mythology
nearby to catch it.

4

In poetry, there are no fixable and final themes, but there is only the experience that comes from the intense and close reading of the words. The poem is a process, a living linguistic reality, and not something like a butterfly with a pin through its body stuck on a board. As one reads, the poem flutters.

~**Duane Locke**

ODE TO PARADOX

(For Silvia Scheibli)

Paradox becomes simple once you gain insight,
then suddenly you feel you should've known it

all along. Like avocado skin wrinkling the bottom
of an ocean green Tupperware compost bowl,

paradox stores maple seeds in its lungs about
to burst after two and a half days of constant rain.

Ah, but your lusty poems shed their ocotillo
blossoms eons ago beneath the fiery nettles

blazing the white-hot sands of the Mojave!

ODE TO TRUTH

(After Juan Ramón Jiménez)

The truth.

Truth creaks a mahogany door, glances
down a wrought iron Andalusian staircase
to young poets lurking below and says, *Truth
regrets to inform you that it's not at home today,
and, therefore, must refrain from any public
appearance that might jeopardize its existence
in an otherwise existential universe.*

Folks well beyond the earshot of truth,
the ones who still read Eliade,
gather fresh sticks
to build a fire.

ODE TO LOVE

(*Life is severe.*)
    ~Duane Locke

The core of love blisters everything,
including a lonely child flailing
in conventional quicksand.

Later that child swats at romantic allies
like fat black flies buzzing the corridors
of adolescent misfortune.

Love frets beneath a turnpike overpass
that shelters Lilith buffing her nails
and swigging melancholy from a paper bag.

Lilith's wine bottle reflects the moonlit
aberration of flesh vulgarized
by humans all across this planet.

Still . . . love is remarkable!

Sometimes love saunters nude through
a room with one bare lightbulb
and a faucet that drips every 18 seconds.

In fact, tonight, love strolls beneath that
one bare bulb while dreaming of a snow
leopard stalking a blue lamb scaling
the icy cliff that Plato chose to ignore.

VARIETAL ODE

I travel from Chile to France
clutching each velvet derivative
by her glass ankle.

Rain pounds the tin roof
of illusion.

Dusk tries to recover,
but it's useless.

Starlit crocodile eyes
invade the wet roots
of October maples.

ODE TO THOUGHTS

I realize that thoughts are amazing things; thoughts themselves are energy.

Some, in fact, are what scientists might call dark matter or something not yet measured but do, nonetheless, affect things already measured or bright matter.

Which means that some thoughts, which haven't quite revealed themselves, do affect other thoughts by carving ruby gashes on their fully-ripened stalks.

Thus, our lives, to some extent, influenced by things we'll never comprehend.

ODE TO LANGSTON HUGHES

You gotta understand,
that's how he lived,
perhaps the first Beat
to strut the sidewalks
of Harlem.

Well, there was Whitman,
then Lorca came along.

But Langston always saw something
unique in a blindfolded world
that tormented him so.

His poems were rubies
smashed against the wall of fate
in a bigoted crap game.

His voice was a crow
stuffed inside the silken breast pocket
of misery.

His poems were shards
of blood spattered
all across the huge white hands
of America.

ODE TO AMNESIA

(For Shasta Vida Britt: 1987-2002)

Goldfinch ignites diamonds
through patio lattice.

Moment of joy!

October—2 AM—distant freight
train like a mosquito burrows
the darkest corridor of my brain.

ODE TO THE ECHO OF SHELLEY

We quote Mary as October maples hiss,
and a crow, from a Japanese maple fifty

feet away, barks across a split-rail fence.
The crow is the Bride of Frankenstein

frozen inside the capitalist brain. We
raise our squat glasses of brandy to

celebrate the black swans of melancholy
as a blithe squirrel, storing acorns

for the russet winter, rustles maple
leaves falling from our dead thoughts.

ODE TO A DREAM

A large stick of patchouli
in the snout
of a ten-foot alligator.

Stick listing,
smoke spiraling.

And that woman pouring a bag
of bone meal
onto a second gator's bottom jaw,
ten-footer
with the eyes of a basset hound.

I'm above
on a ledge
about to crumble
but sturdy
enough to support
the black swans of melancholy
honking my night sky.

Until an alarm,
two feet away,
with scorpion Morse Code tentacles,
burglarizes my dream
this cold October morning.

ODE TO A BROWN WIDOW

Brown widow treads with precision
between two filthy white asbestos shingles.

Her homeless hips dragging dust balls
filled with shredded leaves, fly carcass,
and moth wing while wedging
herself beneath a sliver of darkness.

Behind her tiny head sweeps her archetypal
body with the ease of an ice-skater
carving Figures at the '26 Olympics.

If consciousness really is a virus,
as some folks say,
I wonder if she's immune?

ODE TO GNATS

What is it with gnats and merlot,
gnats and zinfandel?

Some gnats bathe nude
upon the ruby-mirrored surface
of my late afternoon glass of tranquility.

While others are partial
to a tawny summer chardonnay—
no harm there.

Who'd stop them?

When you think about it,
who wouldn't want to daydream
upon a maroon lake,
naked as a jaybird,
rocking a hammock of maple shadows
to keep from drowning?

5

*Imagination is more important than knowledge.
For knowledge is limited to all we now know and
understand, while imagination embraces the entire world,
and all there ever will be to know and understand.*

~Albert Einstein

ODE TO NOTHING

1.
Eight gnats in chardonnay,
floating on their backs,
enjoying the twelfth
of their seventeen days on this earth.

Earth is god;
it's that simple.

So, all we need to know
is how everything else
has existed
still exists
and will exist
till the end of time.

Illusion in Webster's is illustrated
by a white dove with amber eyes
emerging from a black tuxedo sleeve.

Mockingbird's flint wings
slash the blue gravel road.

Warblers, active in late October chill,
await the heel
of a young flamenco dancer
whose walnut hair
and smoky eyes
stare down the baggy flesh
of my wrinkled soul.

But the oriole two yards away
in this ultra-civilized 21st century neighborhood
chirps with abandon
during his 12th month
of a 17-month existence.

2.
Pepper Jack announces
he's the neighborhood's dominant spaniel,
albeit skittish and a bit nippy.

Goldfinch chirps like a child's metal clicker,
one of those annoying toys from the late 1950s
echoing a Florida pink cinderblock house.

Suddenly, there appeared one Palm Beach summer
a terracotta roof
with kitchen saloon doors
and a maid's quarters abandoned
for at least two generations.

Ah, the not-so-good life!

Why couldn't a moon,
say, one of Jupiter's,
be a sister
like Trakl's sister
or Wordsworth's?

Poets have the best sisters.

For that matter, why couldn't arctic wolves
be moons orbiting my imagination
as I step from the shower?

3.
My kinesis is ailing
like a broken leg
bobbing
the hindquarters
of a wild dog of Africa.

Kinesis is an art;
no, I guess it's a science;
see, I don't know;
that's why mine's ailing in the first place.

Who'd ever think that twitching chestnut eyebrows
could replace a verb's delicate
banana-peel bruise?

A bare hip
perched atop a pink wall in Key Largo,
I understand,
but adjectives like aperitifs,
it doesn't make sense.

4.
Well, what would happen if the earth
stopped spinning?

You can't say it's impossible
just because it never has.

So, god is energy produced by the magnetic field
that binds us to our misery?

I wonder, should we introduce god trading cards,
gods from all cultures, all religions?

I'd be willing to flip cards
just to see what miracles transpire.

5.
Sunlight freezes palomino maples
rattling a chilly Canadian wind.

The palms of my hands curl.

The entire earth chatters;
sometimes we hear.

Jesus was a teacher
above all else,
right?

He invented purple.

6.

In Salem, unwitting young women
ate witchcraft in the form
of moldy biscuits,
each one spread by a freshly melted myth.

The devil himself
(in this case *herself*)
blossomed from a tiny seed of rye
called ergot.

That dark speck turned out to be more
powerful than a 2,000-year-old religion.

Animal spirits emerged
from the women's bodies.

Their holy bodies brutalized
by Puritan mythology.

7.

God emerged one day, like he has over millennia,
as Hieronymus Bosch painting demons
on the undersides of eyelids,
a uniquely divine Dark Ages Sistine Chapel.

These demons reemerged one spring morning
from the white mud of ergot flour
baked into steaming loaves relaxing
on angelic racks in abandoned bakeries
at Pont-Saint-Esprit, France, 1951.

8.

I suppose you could say god wears designer sunglasses
that resemble psychedelic poison dart frogs donning

three-piece revolvers or magnolia leaves with
sulfur digesting their yellow-green centers.

9.
O_2 sniffs the white ankles of Turkish tobacco.

10.
These gnats that get into my wine;
when I fish them out,
I can't kill em, you know;
they only want what I do.

So, I sift them gently
onto a ruby fingertip
and watch their wings dry
to flutter away.

Soon they become popular, these gnats,
in their cologne
of merlot, shiraz and sultry chardonnay.

11.
Our neighbor's nylon flag of Santa Claus
snapped by a chilly November wind;
larger American flag above snuffles,
as a mother cat would her kitten,
the back of its orphaned polyester head.

12.
Sea star tentacles
absorb a purple and white mollusk.

13.
There's an ecstasy in melancholy
that cannot be explained.

14.
The kitchen wall clock
hesitates.

That clock's an anchor
with its round brass mirror
slicing and dicing the universe.

15.
*The noose sways for you and
me,* the crooner sings
as he mourns
his wasted life.

He lifts his fork,
and on its five mirrored tips he
shaves his face
foaming
with amnesia

16.
Radiant in black silks,
two ravens share the acorns of
their thoughts.

The moth with pumpkin swirl
the size
of one fingertip
flutters
between vanilla porch light and
the asbestos
white wall
of a dream.

17.
Diamonds are the devil's tears,
my mother said

when I first fell in love.

My beloved's perfume was a tomb.

With black silk strap lilting her left shoulder
she transformed into a wasp inside a harmonica.

Violin mandibles the color of palmetto bugs smashed
beneath an arcade penny-flattening machine . . .

Morphine oozes.

18.
An elephant steps on a land mine.

Her right forefoot hangs like a jellyfish.

A three-legged elephant
crushes a human skull.

Out spurts the ancient religion
that produced the land mine
in the first place.

19.
Earlier, a priest and a cleric carefully positioned pins
and beads of shrapnel
capable of blowing away
competing gods who happen to eavesdrop.

20.
The jade scale fallen from a lightning bug's tail
lands on a cheek
directly below a young woman's eye
leaving a faint charcoal smudge.

The gorgeous zebra eye blinks twice,
then steps from her socket

into a dance club where ice cubes
incubating whiskey tumblers
ignite her charcoal smudge
into rainbow strobe lights.

21.
Quicksilver trickles the tight waist
of an hourglass.

Grasshoppers exchange red and yellow eyelashes.

Stars high above the Everglades
flicker ochre
then green.

The moon crumbles
onto courthouse steps.

The rising sun
has ample time to kill.

22.
Emily Dickinson's frog
spoke to a bog
and said, *I am Caruso,*
who loves the bright stage
while others look on!

Though Emily herself preferred
second-story isolation
while embracing the supple waist
of imagination.

And so it was with Edith Piaf,
Little Sparrow,
eyes squeezed
like two blue spiders,
rustling her cognac voice.

23.
Caressing the waist of an hourglass,
you meet nefarious despots
who permeate the ages.

In fact, so many religions
get marketed by these despots.

It makes you wonder.

24.
Fingertips stroke the sofa's velvet cocoa ridges
shredded by a cat
from the local shelter.

Across the room
a gnome measures the curled bristles of his acrylic brush
against the nude torso of a naïve angel.

His wild acrylic tip sniffs first
her left rib, then left breast
of this red-haired angel,
angel with muscular wings
and crystal eyes intently focused
upon her distant moth of fate.

With one toe curled this gnome's leather moccasin
reaches just beyond the mythical marble platform rising
high above adolescent cotton clouds.

25.
Magnolia buds encased in ice
drip sulfur
onto a just-below-freezing
afternoon.

The afternoon's blue waist
creaks

each time
the wind
has a new thought.

26.
Seaweed washes the ankle
of a bare light bulb
in a chemical warehouse
near Southeast Baltimore.

A guitar provides deliverance
for the golden spoon tilted
above the flame of existence,
flattered, of course, by heavy-breathing
angels surrounding the naked flame
while scrubbing their hands like mantis
philosophers poised
on the brink of epiphany.

27.
I share lunch
with a 98-year-old Bouvier des Flandres.

She leans on one elbow,
silvered and calloused
from years of dreaming upon Berber carpet,
before rising to patrol
the perimeter of her darkness,
sniffing each twisted branch,
each new wild rose petal fallen
at the ankle of a streetlight,
while guarding every corner
of her icy December yard.

28.
A man relates to ashes,
against his better judgment.

Shoulders arise from a sitar's muscular ashes.

Green ashes.

Black ashes,
or fur,
if you prefer.

29.
Onionskin eyelid
twitches when a popular song
imitates a jumbo jet
traveling just below
the whisper of sadness.

30.
We brace ourselves
for spray paint
sprawled across a New Jersey overpass
or subway bridge
above a Brooklyn Greyhound station.

But ashes
are cleansing thoughts.

31.
Through a lace curtain,
a downy woodpecker
scales a thin cherry branch,
grips the branch's shadow
for all he's worth,
for all his icy bougainvillea days,
his favorite bougainvillea flower,
plum,
plus all the adolescent vulgarity

of peach
and white blossoms
to symbolize
a language never spoken.

Somehow memory
provides
a modicum
of relief
when you least
expect
it.

32.
You hear that echo of Blake?

Wolf chased from the pack,
armed against another London winter?

33.
Like a young madonna,

blue as a star tarnished by darkness,

a milkmaid pours grief from a pitcher

before her 16th century townhouse window.

34.
The angel who skips Sunday School
brings us these ashes.

He expects us to discard them
or else find a permanent
Smithsonian solution for their rootless souls.

35.
I don't know
how to tell you

that I love you,
but I imagine, eventually, you'll
get the idea—
our impossible philosophies
wrapping their lips around
maple pods
helicoptering
napalm sunsets.

36.
The planet shivers.

This is not a tooth.
This is not another bored lover
folding four knuckles
against the side of her face.

Spruce tree sheds
icy tears.

Understand, this is not your typical manicured myth,
one offered up as brown spinach
in high school cafeterias.

This is not the Sultan of Congress
stretching his suspenders
for the six o'clock news.

This is not Monday, Wednesday,
or anything remotely manufactured
by Ptolemy.

Young poets creep to readings
down tobacco-stained steps
leading to the basements
of abandoned churches.

Ducking electrical leads and ductwork,
they stand amidst a pool of silence.

37.
So, winter drapes
its icy sleeve
over a mulberry branch
cracking
as spring
enters.

A yellow harmonica
gathers wet leaves
below shattered ice,
geometric eyeballs,
ice of journeys,
ice of symbiotic sleep
meant to replicate desire.

There are many
wandering herds of lovers
lost without direction.

But, oh, how the harmonica's sharp
blades crush brittle solitudes
like teeth culling loved ones
from the herd
while discarding less fortunate ones
destined for utilitarian dreams.

38.
The harmonica breathes melaleuca leaves
between its teeth
like a Tennessee waltz
waiting for death to appear.

Suddenly, death shuffles in,
terrycloth robe, moose-skin slippers.

Wiping existence from his eyes,
death stumbles
from premature slumber.

A coffin slides open.

Magpies fly out;
quicksilver wings refract the moon's nervous
fingertips attempting to steady a brass harmonica
above another dusty dawn.

39.
Pussy willow buds
encased in ice.

Thin willow branches
droop like octopi.

Followed by twelve-thousand Japanese
red maple octopi.

Still, December willows dance,
clacking castanets
above their heads
while raking icy fingers
across the afternoon's blue torso.

40.
A large cognac-colored dog
barks across the snow.

Rain drips from the eaves
as philosophies
about god
and a universal order to things
fall squarely
between a toad's wrinkled gold-striped shoulders.

Cracks in the crevice
gulp icy water
as though it is the
resurrection of joy cocooned

in the University of Georgia library,
1969,
Beethoven's *Ninth*,
Furtwängler,
and a foot of snow,
Athens in single digits.

But, today, it's 32 degrees and pouring water.

41.
Newspaper pages wilted with snow
across the strapless garden.

Two o'clock
and the peeping of a white-throated
sparrow from the den wall clock,
(one hour slow half the year)
dips a single feather
into the gesso of existence.

42.
This morning a raven waddles
below a pine tree near the entrance
of my daughter's school.

Another raven rattles the overhead branches
of a sister pine before escorting
first raven across the road
to an unattended blue spruce.

43.
I'd rather watch a rotting pier
than one of those Hollywood films,
the ones with perfunctory acting
and mechanical plotlines.

I'd opt for a glacier falling on top of me,
a biblical disaster,
one that brings welcome relief
to this antidepressant culture
we've created for ourselves.

44.
Muscular sunlight through embroidered curtains leaves
ocelot spots resembling Mozart's drunken
notations wriggling a wounded minuet.

45.
Were poems ever written with a torch
or a feather?

Ashes staining Indonesian cave walls transfer
a female hand-stenciled myth
to you and me,
just as well as Blake.

While today sunlight switchblading an embroidered
lace curtain delivers serpents, totems, monoliths,
and Alexander's library devoted to this stuff
that nobody else wants.

46.
A politically incorrect co-worker from Chicago
offers a hug
to a veteran of his corporation.

So, *I went out walking through the woods*
the other day
and found irony hiding behind the cabbage palms.

Goblins are the product of a bored mind,
so say philosophers of society stripped
of ego and bodily embarrassments.

You handle a purple incense stick,
as you would a damselfly,
with maximum respect.

If that's traumatic,
think back to childhood—
chest of drawers
glued shut by yellow enamel
dripping from rainbow fables
when white imagination was still
an impetuous illusion.

47.
I hit 40 with a sultry fluke
lilting the infinite.

48.
Pumpkins, tiger gourds, and 19th century grapes
pale as 13th century Japanese women
shouldering water jugs across silkscreens.

Myths, each splinter of every star
a thought
in a godless universe.

49.
Broken key in a lock.

50.
Far from politics,
humans think symbolically.
They weave tapestries
of fantastic
goblins with
curved horns
flowing backwards
as they rescue innocent angels

and peasants bent from exhaustion
with faint beams of light leaking
from their livid imaginations.

You see, this symbolic thinking has some advantages;
for example, if one engages the thermals
of turbulent imagination high
above a paralyzed culture
brimming with archaic myths,
one can finally suckle the delicious corolla
of truth and beauty as Keats described it.

6

Language is the house of Being. Man dwells in this house. Those who think [die Denkenden] and those who create poetry [die Dichtenden] are the custodians of the dwelling.

~Martin Heidegger
(trans. by George Steiner)

(The following is a response to three questions posed to Alan Britt by Ruxandra Cesereanu of the Romanian literary magazine, *Steaua*. The questions: *Why do you write poetry? Who are some of your influences? What's the future of poetry in the US?*)

THE INTUITIVE SOUL

Antonin Artaud once expressed, "I write to get out of hell!" William Blake wrote visionary poetry as a means to expand sensibility through glorious imagination and his five senses. Emily Dickinson turned intense solitude into psychological maps littered with humble emotional roads and avenues of profound insight. Federico García Lorca, whose poems are among the most beautiful ever written, suggested that poetry is a way of expanding human sensibility to its very limits, all the while suggesting that human potential remains a mystery. Duane Locke once wrote poems called "Exorcisms" as a means to exorcise the demons of conventionality from his life. He writes similar poems today, only they're called "Chinese Poet in a Ruined Garden," "Three Glasses of Wine," and "Daphne Poems." Many poets past and present have expanded poetic lexicon through sensitive intelligence. I confess that I read and write poetry for the reasons aforementioned, plus the pure joy of lounging in a Baudelaire prose poem, rising on the wings of Shelley's skylark, or spending an afternoon with Neruda loafing barbershops, mermaids and artichokes.

While I find it more invigorating to write new poems than revisit old ones, moments when slashing a comma or disemboweling an entire stanza also provide joy. Then I wonder who would even notice such diminutive aberrations? So it goes ... the wonder ... the thrill of engaging imagination sometimes soaked in cabernet, sometimes engaged in the peaceful violence of a leopard slug devouring fresh cabbage leaves, while other times stabbed by the magnesium horns of stars prowling a cool autumn night. My world flashes infinite one moment then imprisonment the next. I prefer the infinite universe, which is why I write poems.

    Poetry is for those who love mystery, for those in love with the expansive soul, so it's natural for poets to suspend disbelief long enough to explore the sleepy brain by extending astral tendrils deep into the natural world, thereby bringing us eye to glistening eye with a yellow and black garden spider hovering in the breeze of profound despair. Exhilarating to discover oneself word by word, image by image, between the beautiful hips of a fresh poem. The marriage of imagination and language produces a palpable intellectual and emotional life. This is spiritual existence, one worth living. If poets lose their hunger for the unknown, their infatuation for mystery, then we're doomed to a dehumanized life of commerciality, a life devoid of spirituality.

    The future for US poets is essentially the same as it is for poets everywhere. Embrace the known as though it were the unknown electrified by an expanding sensibility. Embrace truth as we see it? Indeed, we are not politicians; we need not pander or disguise who we are. Poetry is fearless. "As a man is, so he Sees," said Blake.

So, to Romanian poets and to poets everywhere, let's form a bond circling the planet and stay connected through our diverse and often severe environments. We are, after all, sisters and brothers leaving trails of poems like bread crumbs behind to guide folks through the beautiful and cruel universe. Poets have always been creatures of melancholy attempting to find ways into and out of the Black Forest, the hungry womb of existence. Therefore, I invite everyone to enjoy the illuminating poems of Georg Trakl, Yves Bonnefoy, Yannis Ritsos, Miguel Hernández, and Silvia Scheibli. Their poems are flaming mushrooms below our dark feet. Meanwhile, I'll continue to drop embers of poems like bread crumbs from the turned-out pockets of my intuitive soul.

NOTES

Section 1: Epigraph by Pablo Neruda from his poem, "Tonight I Can Write the Saddest Lines" from his book *Twenty Love Poems and a Song of Despair/Veinte poemas de amor y una canción desesperada* published in Santiago, Chile: 1924

Page 20: From "Geronimo's Cadillac," words and music by Michael Murphy and Charles Quarto from *The Road* by Johnny Rivers, Atlantic Records, Los Angeles: 1974

Section 2: Epigraph by Pablo Neruda from his poem, "Ode to Things" from his book *Odes to Common Things*, translated by Ken Krabbenhoft, Bullfinch/Little Brown & Co.: 1994

Section 3: Epigraph by E.S. Shaffer on Samuel Taylor Coleridge from *Kubla Khan and The Fall of Jerusalem: The Mythological School in Biblical Criticism and Secular Literature 1770-1880*, Cambridge University Press, Cambridge, Massachusetts and London, England: 1975

Section 4: Epigraph by Duane Locke from his Introduction to *The Immanentist Anthology*, edited by Duane Locke and Harry Smith, The Smith Press/Villiers, Ltd., Brooklyn, NY/London, England: 1973

Page 61: Quote from Duane Locke in conversation with Alan Britt circa 1995

Section 5: Epigraph by Albert Einstein on 1929 October 26, *The Saturday Evening Post*, "What Life Means to Einstein: An Interview by George Sylvester Viereck," Start Page 17, Quote on Page 117, Column 1, Saturday Evening Post Society, Indianapolis, Indiana. (Verified on microfilm)

Section 6: Epigraph by Martin Heidegger from his "Letter on Humanism" translated by George Steiner: 1946 [Letter on Humanism (German: Brief über den Humanismus) refers to a famous letter written by Martin Heidegger in December 1946 in response to a series of questions by Jean Beaufret (10 November 1946) about the development of French existentialism. Heidegger reworked the letter for publication in 1947. He distanced himself from Sartre's position and existentialism in general in this letter.]

Mel Ramos's art has been curated in almost every major gallery on the planet and currently hangs in some of the world's finest museums. His influence on contemporary art is immeasurable and commensurate with that of other pop artists such as Andy Warhol, Roy Lichtenstein, Claes Oldenburg, Jasper Johns, James Rosenquist, and Yayoi Kusama. *Guilty Pleasures* is the first book that features a painting by Mel Ramos on its cover.

Mel taught at California State University, Hayward, CA (1966-1997) and was Artist-in-Residence at Syracuse University, Syracuse, NY (1970) and at the University of Wisconsin, Madison, WI (1973). In 1986 he was awarded both a National Endowment for the Arts Visual Artists Fellowship Grant and a United States-France Exchange Fellowship. Below is a selected list of Public Collections of Mel's art.

Albertina, Vienna, Austria
Art Bank, U.S. Department of State, Washington D.C.
Art Gallery of Ontario, Toronto, Canada
Corcoran Gallery of Art, Washington D.C.
Crocker Art Museum, Sacramento, CA
H.M. de Young Museum, San Francisco
Guggenheim Museum, New York, NY
Hirshhorn Museum and Sculpture Garden, Washington D.C.
Hamburger Kunsthalle, Hamburg, Germany
Indianapolis Museum, Indianapolis, IN
Kunsthaus, Darmstadt, Germany
Los Angeles County Museum of Art, Los Angeles, CA
Museum of Contemporary Art, Chicago
Museum of Contemporary Art, Los Angeles
Museum of Contemporary Art, Skopje, Macedonia
Museum of Modern Art, New York, NY
Museum Moderner Kunst, Vienna, Austria
National Gallery of Art, Washington, DC
Neue Galerie Stadt Aachen, Aachen, Germany

Gabriel Navar is a contemporary, professional California artist, poet and college arts educator living and working in the San Francisco Bay Area. He is fully engaged in his work and dedicated to producing provocative, relevant, figurative work with a "pop-surrealist-socio-political sensibility," as well as with a "web-based, social-media awareness." His image-making through words, lines, textures and colors are truly all about the "urgency" for making images (as well as a passion for and working with art materials) and, thematically and philosophically-speaking, about this great and often absurd human theater we are currently living! For over twenty years, image-making for Navar has been a passion and avenue for exploring experiences, dreams and preoccupations, including issues of our dependence on technology, consumer culture, relationships, spirituality, politics, and the human "theater."

Navar has always enjoyed making images not only through drawing and painting but also through poetry. He has been writing in a sort of "stream of consciousness," "automatic writing" approach for many, many years. It was not until the late 1980s, early 1990s, however, that he started to write and paint seriously and with a sense of direction. Soon after Navar completed his studies with Mel Ramos in the early 1990s, Navar assisted and aided Ramos in his studio in a variety of tasks. Not long after, due to a colorful variety of circumstances, Navar began to exhibit with his mentor Ramos nationally and abroad. The enthusiasm and joy for creating continues for Navar.

Photo by Charles P. Hayes

I grew up in southeastern Florida where hot summer days sizzled and summer nights pressed jasmine lips against my frosted bedroom jalousies. An aspiring athlete, I wanted to play for the Milwaukee Braves—I thought Hank Aaron was poetry in motion. Anyway, in high school I was songwriter for a garage band and later morphed into a college freshman writing poetry before eventually finding myself a founding member of poets and artists known as the Immanentists. Somewhat eclectic, we were a blend of European Surrealists with a Native American sensibility believing that through language and acrylic paint we could attain spiritual fusion with the natural world. Years later, I drove a yellow Ryder truck from Tampa to Baltimore to attend the graduate Writing Seminars at Johns Hopkins University where I made a beeline to the National Gallery in DC to marvel at the wondrous creations by Rembrandt, Vermeer, Monet, Manet, and Odilon Redon. Baltimore became my heaven with snow. Inspired by Andrew Marvell, William Blake, Walt Whitman, Federico García Lorca, Pablo Neruda, Sándor Kányádi, plus countless others, I now write poems about anything and everything.

Along the way I've learned that to write poetry is to love, and to love is to write poetry.

—Alan Britt

Alan has been nominated for the 2021 International Janus Pannonius Prize awarded by the Hungarian Centre of PEN International for excellence in poetry from any part of the world. Previous nominated recipients include Lawrence Ferlinghetti, Charles Bernstein and Yves Bonnefoy. He has published 21 books of poetry and served as Art Agent for Andy Warhol Superstar, the late great Ultra Violet, while often reading poetry at her Chelsea, New York studio. A graduate of the Writing Seminars at Johns Hopkins University, Alan currently teaches English/Creative Writing at Towson University.

PUBLICATIONS BY ALAN BRITT

Books

Guilty Pleasures
Emergency Room
Optical Illusions
Dream Highway
Gunpowder for Single-ball Poems
Ode to Nothing/Óda a semmihez (bilingual) Translated into Hungarian by Paul Sohar
Violin Smoke/Hegedűfüst (bilingual) Translated into Hungarian by Paul Sohar
Lost Among the Hours
Parabola Dreams (with Silvia Scheibli)
Alone with the Terrible Universe
Greatest Hits
Hurricane
Vegetable Love
Vermilion
Infinite Days
Amnesia Tango
Bodies of Lightning
The Afternoon of the Light
I Suppose the Darkness Is Ours
Ashes in the Flesh
I Ask for Silence, Also

Anthologies (Editor)

We Are You: Poetry
Alianza: 5 U.S. Poets in Ecuador
Mantras: An Anthology of Immanentist Poetry

Poetry Journal (Editor)

Black Moon: Poetry of Imagination

Editor-in-Chief/Poetry Editor/Associate Editor

We Are You Project International
The Loch Raven Review
Ethos Literary Journal

Miscellaneous

Poetry and the Concept of Maya by David Churchill
    (Based upon the poetry of Alan Britt)

Access Road Studios (ARS) supports healing and expansion of the human spirit!

Future creative projects by **ARS** will include music and spoken word CDs and DVDs, plus books of poetry, fiction and nonfiction.

All books by Alan Britt are available through Magical Jeep Distributing:
www.magicaljeep.com/shop/britt/10

Guilty Pleasures and other books by Alan Britt are also available on Amazon plus many independent bookstores across the US, including the Shivastan Bookshop & Art Gallery in Woodstock, New York and the Katsea Gallery in Towson, Maryland (see ads).

SHIVASTAN BOOKSHOP & ART GALLERY

NEW, USED, & RARE BOOKS + ART, JEWELRY, CRAFTS

GREAT GIFTS FROM INDIA & NEPAL

6 SGT RICHARD QUINN DR/HILLCREST AVE
WOODSTOCK – ORANGE CABIN IN BACK

OPEN 1 to 6pm EVERYDAY

SHIVASTAN BOOKSHOP & ART GALLERY
6 Hillcrest Avenue/Sgt. Richard Quinn Drive
(Up Neher Street from Tinker Street next to the
American Legion in the back)
Woodstock, NY 12498
(PH: 845-684-0407)
(www.shivastan.com)

katsea gallery

1 W. Pennsylvania Avenue
Towson, MD 21204
at the corner of York Road and Pennsylvania Avenue
in the Towson Commons
Artwork by Nico G Silk-Art

The gallery has mixed media, sculptures, fine art photography, abstract paintings, landscape, surrealist and representational oil paintings, plus a book stall for poetry and fiction. The gallery also hosts monthly poetry readings.

To order through the website there is a link to accept payments as well as pay by installments. All information available via the website's online store: www.katseagallery.com

www.ingramcontent.com/pod-product-compliance
Lightning Source LLC
Chambersburg PA
CBHW030042100526
44590CB00011B/301